Single & Relationships
God—Family—Friends
Work—Romance

Individual Devotion
Weekly Small Group
(31 Days to 5 weeks to 31 weeks)

Plus small group instruction and leaders guide.

Dick Purnell
Kris Swiatocho

Published by:
Yes! Marketing and Design Services, Garner, NC
www.YesMarketingandDesign.com

SINGLES AND RELATIONSHIPS
God, Family, Friends, Work, Romance

Copyright ©2011-2022 Dick Purnell and Kris Swiatocho
Published by Yes! Marketing & Design Services
638 Spartanburg Hwy, Suite 70-113
Hendersonville, NC 28792
www.YesMarketingandDesign.com

ISBN-13:
978-1544142951

ISBN-10:
1544142951

All rights reserved: No part of this publication may be reproduced, stored in a retrieval systems, or transmitted in any form or by any means—electronic, mechanical, digital, photocopy, recording, or any other—except for brief quotations in printed reviews, without the prior permission of the publisher.

Printed in the United States of America

Unless otherwise indicated, all Scripture quotations are taken from the HOLY BIBLE, NEW INTERNATIONAL VERSION®, NIV®. Copyright©1973, 1984 by the International Bible Society. Used by permission of Zondervan. All rights reserved.

Table of Contents

What is a *Real* Relationship?...5

Get Ready for Lots of Surprises..9

My Covenant with God...11

My Prayer..12

Plan for Meeting Daily with God..14

Doing This Experiment With Others 17

Section #1 (Days 1-15) Building Relationships God's Way............19

Section #2 (Days 16-31) Going to a Deeper Level...........................51
    in Your Relationships

Keep Going—and Growing...85

The Most Important Thing I Learned About....................................89
    Relationships (Kris Swiatocho)

If You Want to Get Married (Dick Purnell).......................................91

How to Lead a Group of Singles to Experience................................93
    Real Relationships

Weekly Group Participation Outline..97

What is a *Real* Relationship?

What does a real relationship look like? Actually, it depends on who is defining a real relationship.

Let's start with you. How are your relationships? You'd probably answer that some are good, some okay, some not-so-good, and some strained or hostile—quite a mixture. The trouble is, for most people, relationships keep changing—some by the day or hour.

Before we begin our 31-Day Experiment, let's take a brief inventory of your relationship history by asking a few questions:

- Have you experienced disappointments with the people in your life?

- Do you know that there's a need for improvement in your relationships with others?

- Can you think of a relationship that you thought was pretty good at once, but then the relationship suddenly ended…and you wondered why?

- Do you have lots of acquaintances but no real friends?

- Do you feel like no one really knows the inside you?

- Do you sometimes get so irritated with someone that you flare-up? As a result, do you then feel uncomfortable around this person?

- If a family member or friend were to spread rumors about you that hurt deeply, would you wonder how others could believe such lies about you?

- If you have been with one person for a long time, did you start off well and then find you and your partner drifting apart...and now you feel like the relationship is over? Do you feel angry and/or depressed about this?

Most people answer yes to some or all of these questions during their lifetime. But when we go through hard times in our relationships (or lack of them), we can be so focused on the pain involved that we can't see how to mend the rift and return to enjoying a real relationship.

The world (through the media and society) has various definitions for a relationship. The belief is that each of us decides what is best for us...so, if someone likes you, you like them back. But if the person displeases you or hurts you in some way, then you are justified in getting revenge, or at a minimum, ending the relationship.

Did you know that the Roman procurator Pontius Pilate, who was responsible for the death of Christ, had a friend? In the heat of a near riot, when the people were shouting for Christ's crucifixion, Pilate was reluctant to turn Jesus over to the riotous mob. He was trying to decide if he should let this innocent man go free. When the frenzied masses realized he was considering this, they should out to Pilate, "If you let this man go, you are no friend of Caesar. Anyone who claims to be a kind [meaning Jesus] opposes Caesar" (John 19:12).

That made Pilate's decision much easier. He quickly decided to choose friendship with Caesar instead of with Jesus. What an appalling choice! But as hideous as the consequences were, there was one bright spot for Pilate. "That day Herod and Pilate became friends – before this, they had been enemies" (Luke 23:12). The Jews hated Herod (ruler of Galilee, the area north of Jerusalem). He was an evil man who murdered John the Baptist after John confronted Herod for illegally marrying his brother Philip's wife. Even Jesus referred to Herod as "that fox" because of his deceitfulness and evil (Luke 13:32). Herod and Pilate became friends – what a pair. How would you define their relationship?

God has a very different perspective on relationships. This perspective all starts with Him. Centuries after he lived, Abraham was called "God's friend" (James 2:23). Does your heart yearn to become a friend of God?

Jesus described friendship this way, "My command is this: Love each other as I have loved you. Greater love has no one than this that he lay down his life for his friends. You are my friends if you do what I command. I no longer call you servants because a servant does not know his master's business. Instead, I have called you friends, for everything that I learned from my Father I have made known to you" (John 15:12-15).

A true understanding of how real relationships work begins with friendship with God. How much do you want to know God as your friend? A superficial or insincere answer will bring emptiness. Just like superficial friendships, treating the Lord with neglect or impatience will never satisfy the craving of your soul for connection on the deepest level – something that can never be filled with an early relationship of any kind.

You probably are very busy and have lots of demands on your time. But do you really want to take the time each day to meet personally with your heavenly Father? If you don't have time for God, you will miss the greatest relationship of life – and you'll miss learning how to relate to others in a genuinely satisfying way.

God is so gracious and wants you to know Him. But Jesus did let people walk away from Him. Jesus attracted only those who desired truth and a real relationship with Him. So, too, the Lord will not force you to meet with Him as His friend...the choice is yours.

If you do make a choice to come closer to God, He will break down between the two of you. But He never stops with just a vertical relationship with Him. He always motivates you to improve your horizontal relationships – with those around you, both friends and strangers. When your heart aches for Him, He gives you a desire to love others.

So real relationships emanate from a real God who loves us with real sacrificial love demonstrated through Christ. Do you want your relationships to change from superficial to saturated with God's love? Do you want Christ's forgiveness to fill your heart and mend severed ties? Do you want to Holy Spirit's power to break hardness, hostility, and hatred?

If so, then get ready for 31 days of adventure. If you're serious about this 31-Day Experiment, you will witness dramatic changes in your heart and your actions. You may be tempted to quit – but please don't. You may get too busy – if so, then slow down, but press on. You may find rationalizations to procrastinate and take some days off. If that occurs, then pray. You may face obstacles along the way...but you can overcome them all.

What then is a real relationship? It's one founded on, saturated with, and motivated by the living God.

If you want relationships like that, you're ready to begin Day 1 of this Experiment.

Get Ready for *Lots* of Surprises

You can begin a month-long adventure relating to people, using the Bible as your guidebook and the Holy Spirit as your counselor. Below are the titles and topics you will be studying for the next 31 days. Go down the list and read each one out loud.

Then ask your heavenly Father to begin deepening your friendship with Him. Tell Him you are serious about changing your relationships to conform to His will. Expect God to work in your heart and life actively. This is a prayer He delights to answer.

Section #1 – Building Relationships God's Way
1. Friends are Great, but the Lord Is My All
2. The Most Important Relationship You Will Ever Have
3. Truth and Commitment Form the Foundation
4. Loyalty Binds Different People Together
5. You Have More Potential Friends Than You Think
6. The Fun of Being Together
7. Corrupt Friends Bring Devastating Results
8. Taking the Initiative to Heal Broken Relationships
9. Don't Listen to Some Friends
10. Bad Friends Can Influence You to Do Bad Things
11. Praying with Your Heart
12. Becoming a Peacemaker Rather Than a Troublemaker
13. Open Your Heart and Then Your Home
14. Encourage Each Other
15. Handling Loneliness

Section #2 – Going to a Deeper Level in Your Relationships

16. Getting Along with Different People
17. Getting Along with Difficult People
18. We All Have the Same Purpose
19. Don't Pattern Your Relationships After the World
20. We All Need Kind Correction – But Do You Want It?
21. Forgiven So You Can Forgive
22. What Do You Have in Common?
23. It's What You Have Right Now That Counts
24. A Whole New Dimension to Your Love
25. Become a Peacemaker
26. Reconciliation is Hard, but the Right Things
27. Two Kinds of Friends – Love the One and Shun the Other
28. Mental and Physical Discipline Can Produce Holy Living
29. Overflowing Joy in Giving
30. Hang in There for the Long Haul
31. When the Heat Comes, Fire Up!

My Covenant *with* God

I commit myself before God to do this experiment, *Singles and Relationships,* for the next 31 days (or_____weeks) . Today, I make a covenant with the Lord Jesus to:

1. Spend 20 to 30 minutes each day in Bible study, prayer, and writing out my thoughts and plans.

2. Ask at least one other Christian to pray daily for me that the experiment will help me understand and apply God's plan for my life (that person may want to do the experiment along with me so we can share together what we are learning).

3. Attend a church each week where the Word of God is taught.

Signed _____

Date _____

My Prayer *(31 Day Experiment)*

Dear Heavenly Father,

My creator and sustainer. You are my God, and I am truly thankful.

From the beginning of human life on earth, you designed us to desire relationships – especially with You deeply.

Thank You for loving the world so much that You sent Your Son, Jesus, to reestablish our relationship with You after our sin separated us. Jesus is my Savior, my Lord, and my friend. I have been reconciled to You through faith in Him, and I am eternally grateful.

I want my relationship with You to grow stronger and my trust in You to deepen. However, I fall short of spending quality time with You so many times, building that relationship.

Father, I ask for Your forgiveness and guidance to do better. As I spend time each day doing this 31-Day Experiment, draw me closer that I may know You better and love You more. Teach me the things You want me to learn. It's my greatest desire that I become more like You each day.

Dear Lord, change my human relationships so that I treat others as You would want me to. Strengthen my friendships. Heal strained relationships and soften hardened hearts.

And if there is someone You have designed for me to marry, I pray that our relationship will be filled with love for You and based fully on Your Word. Lead us together in Your time and in Your way.

Thank You, Father, for Your truth, direction, and living presence in my life. I am so glad I am a child of Yours.

I look forward to the next 31 days with great expectations.
In the name of the Lord Jesus Christ. Amen!

Signed: _____ Date:_____

My Prayer *(Small Group-5 weeks or more)*

Dear Heavenly Father,

My creator and sustainer. You are my God, and I am truly thankful.

From the beginning of human life on earth, you designed us to desire relationships – especially with You deeply.

Thank You for loving the world so much that You sent Your Son, Jesus, to reestablish our relationship with You after our sin separated us. Jesus is my Savior, my Lord, and my friend. I have been reconciled to You through faith in Him, and I am eternally grateful.

I want my relationship with You to grow stronger and my trust in You to deepen. However, I fall short of spending quality time with You so many times, building that relationship.

Father, I ask for Your forgiveness and guidance to do better. As I spend time each day doing this 31-Day Experiment, draw me closer that I may know You better and love You more. Teach me the things You want me to learn. It's my greatest desire that I become more like You each day.

Dear Lord, change my human relationships so that I treat others as You would want me to. Strengthen my friendships. Heal strained relationships and soften hardened hearts.

And if there is someone You have designed for me to marry, I pray that our relationship will be filled with love for You and based fully on Your Word. Lead us together in Your time and in Your way.

Thank You, Father, for Your truth, direction, and living presence in my life. I am so glad I am a child of Yours.

I look forward to the next 31 days with great expectations.
In the name of the Lord Jesus Christ. Amen!

Signed: _____ Date: _____

Plan for Meeting Daily *with* God

Preparation for Each Day

1. **Equipment.** Obtain a translation of the Bible that you enjoy reading. If you want to use the same translation used in this book, look at the New International Version (NIV). Get a pen to record in this book or journal. Journal your thoughts, answers to prayers and plans.

2. **Time.** Chose a specific half hour each day to spend with the Lord. Pick the time of day this is best for you – when your heart is most receptive to meeting with God.

3. **Place.** Find a particular spot where you can clear your mind of distractions and focus your full attention of God's Word. Choose to turn off your phone.

Read (10-20 Minutes)

1. Pray earnestly before you begin. Ask the Lord to teach you what He desires you to learn.

2. Read the entire passage that is the selection for the day.

3. Read it again, looking for important statements about God and His working in a believer's life.

4. Make written notes on the following:

   Sections A and B – Study the passage thoroughly to answer the questions. Observe what God says about Himself and what He wants you to know about developing dynamic, God-centered relationships. As you discover more of His truth, your understanding of God's purposes for you will increase.

   Section C – Write out your personal responses to the Scripture you have studied. How, specifically, will you apply the lessons you have learned to your life?

5. Choose a verse from the passage you just read that is especially meaningful to you. Copy it onto an index card and read it several times during the day. Think about its meaning and impact on your life. Memorize it when you have free mental time; for example, when you are getting ready in the morning, while you are standing in line, taking a coffee break, waiting for class to begin, going through your exercise routine, or walking somewhere.

Need (5 Minutes)

1. Pray that the Lord will give you insight into your own life.

2. Decide what your most pressing personal need is that day. It may be the same as on previous days, or it may be different.

3. Write down your request. The more specific your request, the more precise the answer will be.

4. Earnestly pray each day for God's provision. As you progress through the experiment, exercise your developing faith. Trust God for big things.

5. When the Lord meets your need, record the date and how He did it. Periodically review God's wonderful provisions, and thank Him often for His faithfulness. This will greatly increase your faith and confidence in Him.

6. At the end of the month, review all the answers to your prayers. Rejoice in God's goodness to you. Keep praying for the requests that still need answers.

Deed (5 Minutes)

1. Pray for the Lord's guidance and wisdom to help another person during the day. Try to apply the particular passage you have just studied.

2. Take the initiative to express God's wonderful love to someone. Be a servant. Someone has said, "Behind every face there is a drama going on." Tap into at least one person's drama each day. Serve that person and share what you are learning.

3. As you help a needy person, tell him or her about your faith in Christ. Here are some suggestions for helping someone:

   a. Provide a meal.
   b. Take care of someone's children for an evening.
   c. Help a friend study for a school test.
   d. Do yard work with a neighbor.
   e. Write an encouraging letter.
   f. Start a Bible study.
   g. Teach someone a sports activity, mechanical skill, or something else you enjoy.
   h. Assist in moving household possessions.
   i. Take someone out to lunch and listen to the needs expressed.
   j. Fix something for a neighbor.
   k. Show interest in another person's interests.
   l. Give an honest compliment.
   m. Pray with a friend about a need.
   n. Contribute money to a mission's cause.
   o. Visit someone in the hospital or at a retirement home.

4. Later, record the details of how the Holy Spirit used you this day. This will increase your confidence to reach out to others. Thank the Lord Jesus for expressing His love and compassion to others through you.

Application
1. Write down your thoughts about how you can put into practice specific instructions and ideas found in the passage.

2. Devise a plan to implement your ideas.

Last Thing in the Evening

1. **Read** – Look at the passage again, looking for additional ideas about singles and relationships.

2. **Need** – Pray again for your concerns. Thank the Lord that He will answer in His way and in His time. Expect the Spirit of the Living God to strengthen you in your walk with Him.

3. **Deed** – Record how God guided you to accomplish something for Him.

4. **Application** – Review what you learned today. Look for further biblical insight to help you apply the passage to your life.

Doing This Experiment with Others
(Small Group/Sunday School Class)

Singles & Relationships is designed to be done in either 31 straight days, 5 weeks or 31 weeks.

Pray frequently for one another that you will learn more about the Lord and how to live for Him. Encourage one another to be disciplined and faithful in completing the experiment. Share what you are learning and how the heavenly Father is working in your lives.

Optional formats:

- **One-on-one:** This is a great study to do one-on-one, especially with someone who is searching for accountability in their various relationships of family, friends, work, romantic and God.

- **Group:** Church, ministry, home or work, Sunday school/small group See the section on page 93 "*How to Lead a Group of Singles to Experience Real Relationship*" for practical suggestions.

  5 weeks:
  –Week one: Introduction, share how to do the study, go over and sign the covenant, talk about expectations, have an icebreaker or get to know you exercise, and pray. Be sure to let them know what days to read and do before the next week.
  –Week two: You will go over Days 1-7
  –Week three: You will go over Days 8-15
  –Week four: You will go over Days 16-23
  –Week five: You will go over Days 24-31

  Note: Optional additional week to have a group party/dinner and share testimonials.

More than 5 weeks:
-Week one: Introduction, share how to do the study, go over and sign the covenant, talk about expectations, have an icebreaker or get to know you exercise, and pray. Be sure to let them know what days to read and do before the next week.

Option 1: You can take as much time as you like to do this study. Instead of doing 7 days per week, you can opt to do less, extending the study into 8 weeks. You would have the same introduction week but then you would discuss Days 1-5, 6-10, 11-15, 16-20, 21-25, 26-30 for weeks 2-7; leaving the last day for the last week.

Option 2: You can teach different days based on the category such as:
-Week 1: Days 1, 7, 10, 27 (Friends)
-Week 2: Days 12, 14, 25, 28 (Struggle)

31 Weeks:
You can also use each of the 31 Days for 31 weeks of teaching. But as the leader/teacher, we encourage you to add additional scriptures, bring props, add stories, testimonials, and follow-up the application to get the most out of the study. *See our section in the back on additional leadership ideas.*

Singles and Relationships

Section #1 – Building Relationships God's Way

Days 1-15

Date _____

Day 1

Friends Are Great, but the Lord Is My All
Psalm 62

Key Verses: Find rest, O my soul, in God alone; my hope comes from his. He alone is my rock and my salvation; he is my fortress, I will not be shaken (Psalm 2:5-6).

Today's Focus:
This book is about building dynamic, satisfying, fun – and real – relationships...and how to maintain and strengthen them. Yes, people will sometimes do or say things that will disappoint you. In the critical hour, you may be rejected, misunderstood, or left by yourself.

If you look to humans as the source for your ultimate fulfillment and sense of well-being you will be disappointed. Instead, place your life and heart in God's hands.

Read: Praise God that He is the majestic Lord who loves you.

A. Write down all the words that complete this sentence – God is my...

B. What two things did David hear about the Lord?

C. My soul finds rest in God alone because:

Need:
Ask God to move your dependence from people to Him. My greatest need today is:

God's answer to my prayer came on _____ (date) by this means:

Deed: Pray for others who are depending on themselves or others to find happiness. Today, dear God, guide my steps so that I will meet people who are lonely or discouraged so that I can:

Application
Read Psalm 2 out loud. Then read it again, but this time, make it a prayer. If you have a tendency to complain about your "lot in life," thank God He is your sufficiency. If you love your life, thank God He is the Author of life.

Date _____

Day 2

The Most Important Relationship You Will Ever Have

Romans 5:1-11

Key Verse: For if, when we were God's enemies, we were reconciled to him through the death of his Son, how much more, having been reconciled, shall we be saved through his life! (Romans 5:10)

Today's Focus:
It all starts with God. Because of your sin (everyone has sinned), your relationship with God has been severed. To choose to have a meaningful relationship with Him is the greatest decision you will ever make.

Read: Pray to be reconciled to God.

A. How did we obtain this relationship with God?

B. Why did God want to make us His friends?

C. I want to be a friend of God because:

Need:
Pray for your friendship with God. My greatest need today is:

God's answer to my prayer came on _____ (date) by this means:

Deed:
Pray for opportunities to strengthen your friendship with God.
I will trust God to:

Application
How does it feel to know that God wants a friendship with you? You don't have to wait till you're married or have all the material possessions or the perfect job. He wants a relationship with you right now, today! If you have not given your life to God or you are not sure, ray and put your faith in Him today. Here is a simple prayer: "Lord Jesus, I believe You are God and that You died for my sins. I receive You as my Savior and Lord. Thank You for reconciling me with the heavenly Father. Amen."

Date _____

Day 3

Truth and Commitment Form The Foundation
Genesis 6:1-22

Key Verse: This is the account of Noah. Noah was a righteous man, blameless among the people of his time, and he walked with God (Genesis 6:9).

Today's Focus:
You probably have many different kinds of relationships – with parents, siblings, relatives, coworkers, acquaintances, school buddies, and longtime friends. But a close relationship with God is more important than all of them. Noah walked with God, and he can show you how to do the same.

Read: Pray for a close relationship with God.

A. Why did God choose Noah?

B. What do you think Noah did to walk with God?

C. I believe my relationship with God can be closer by:

Need:
Pray to be responsive and obedient to God. My greatest need

God's answer to my prayer came on _____ (date) by this means:

Deed:
Pray for someone that you desire to be closer to, whether it is a friend or a romantic interest. In order for this to happen, what must I do first?

Application
Commitment – what is that exactly? Sometimes it's difficult for us to use the word. We value our independence – it has become one of the highest virtues of our culture. But independence brings consequences we don't like – loneliness, insecurity, isolation.

When you commit your heart and life to God, He holds you tighter than you hold Him. Find out about His commitment to you in Romans 8.

Date _____

Day 4

Loyalty Binds Different People Together
2 Samuel 23:8-39

Key Verse: These are the names of David's mighty men (2 Samuel 23:8).

Today's Focus:
David is given credit for conquering his enemies and establishing the nation of Israel. But he didn't do it by himself. He had his mighty men, men who were fiercely loyal to him. Brave, yes. Committed, yes. Their loyalty to one another made them strong against all the enemies of Israel.

Read:
Praise God that He is the "glue" that binds us together.

A. What great exploits did these mighty men accomplish?

B. Why do you think David, at the end of his life, gave such honor to these men?

C. I want to build a group of loyal friends so that:

Need:
Great Sovereign Lord, give me a strong group of friends who are committed to one another. My greatest need today is:

God's answer to my prayer came on _____(date) by this means:

Deed:
Sovereign Lord, guide me to show honor toward my loyal friends. Write down a list of your friends and some ideas about how to show your appreciation for their friendship.

Application
Reread today's passage and look for the names of David's mighty men. Look them up in a Bible concordance to learn what other great things they accomplished. Discover what motivated these men to stand with David in threatening and distressful times.

Date _____

Day 5

You Have More Potential Friends Than You Think

Galatians 3:1-29

Key Verses: Now that faith has come, we are no longer under the supervision of the law. You are all sons of God through faith in Christ Jesus, for all of you who were baptized into Christ have been clothed with Christ (Galatians 3:25-27).

Today's Focus:
Having common interests brings people together. The most significant basis for friendship is our faith. That is the common ground of all who believe in Him. We are in one family because we are His children through faith.

Read:
Thank God you are His child.

A. Contrast characteristics of the law with Christ.
The Law   Christ

B. What happens when you put your faith in Christ?

C. I know that I am a child of God because:

Need:
Pray for greater determination to live by faith. Father, as Your child, I come to You asking for Your provision for my greatest need today:

God's answer to my prayer came on _____ (date) by this means:

Deed:
Pray for others to put their faith in Christ. Because of my faith, Christ has given me new life, and I will tell others today that:

Application
When people have the same heavenly Father through faith in Christ, they have the same promises. List the characteristics you are looking for in people with whom you want to become friends. How does faith in Christ unite individuals?

Date _____

Day 6

The Fun of Being Together
Romans 15:14-33

Key Verse: I plan to do so when I go to Spain. I hope to visit you while passing through and to have you assist me on my journey there, after I have enjoyed your company for a while (Romans 15:24).

Today's Focus:
Paul planned to just stop off in Rome on his way to Spain. He wanted to visit with his friends. Dynamic relationships like this are attractive and refreshing. You bring a deep joy to each other, and the time passes quickly. As you pray for each other, everyone is brought closer to the Lord.

Read:
Thank the Lord He has a specific purpose for you.

A. Why did Paul want to visit the Christians in Rome?

B. What types of things brought Paul joy?

C. When I get together with my friends, I want to:

Need:
Lord Jesus Christ, my greatest need today is:

God's answer to my prayer came on _____ (date) by this means:

Deed:
Pray earnestly for specific friends of yours. Because of the grace God gave me, I believe the Lord has given me a duty to:

Application
Do you believe true joy will come from having a spouse? Why or why not? Conduct an informal survey among other single adults. Ask them what has brought them real joy and fulfillment. Compare their answers with passages in the Bible (for example, read Psalm 63) that reveal the source of lasting fulfillment.

Date _____

Day 7

Corrupt Friends Bring Devastating Results

Genesis 37:1-36

Key Verse: when his brothers saw that their father loved him more than any of them, they hated him and could not speak a kind word to him (Genesis 37:4).

Today's Focus:
Within a group of people, individuals can get jealous of each other and even hateful. When a person is the focus of gossip or sarcasm, divisions occur resulting in anger, hurt feelings, and even harm.

Read:
Praise the heavenly Father the He loves you and has a purpose for your life.

A. What emotions did Joseph's brothers feel toward him?

B. What did they do to him as a result of their feelings?

C. Because I don't want friends who act like that, I will:

Need:
Lord Jesus, help me build friends who are true companions and who love You. My greatest need today is:

God's answer to my prayer came on _____ (date) by this means:

Deed:
Dear Lord, guide me to people today who need Your comfort and peace. When I talk with people who have been hurt by others, I want to share with them:

Application
God has a lot to say about gossip, slander, and malicious treatment of others. Start with Colossians 3:1-17 to understand God's admonitions about good relationships. Get a Bible concordance and look up these words: anger, gossip, grumbling, and malice. Look for ideas about how to counteract the negative things people can do to others.

Date _____

Day 8

Taking the Initiative To Heal Broken Relationships
Genesis 45:1-28

Key Verses: Then Joseph said to his brothers, "Come close to me." When they had done so, he said, "I am your brother Joseph, the one you sold into Egypt! And now, do not be distressed and do not be angry with yourselves for selling me here, because it was to save lives that God sent me ahead of you" (Genesis 45:4-5).

Today's Focus:
Joseph has every reason to hate his brothers for selling him into slavery. But instead he showed kindness toward them. Only God can do that in a person's heart.

Read:
Thank God He reunites estranged people.

A. What did Joseph believe about God and His working through circumstances of life?

B. How did Joseph show he truly loved his brothers?

C. I want the Lord to change my heart toward people who have hurt me because:

Need:
Jesus, you are the Great Physician. Heal my heart and my strained relationships. My greatest need today is:

God's answer to my prayer came on _____(date) by this means:

Deed:
Dear Jesus, help me to reach out to people that need Your healing power and comfort. Write down the key ideas from Joseph's attitudes and actions in this passage.

Application
The reality is that you cannot force or manipulate the reconciliation you seek. Pray about your desires and take the steps to try to bring healing into difficult relationships. Ask others to pray for you and give suggestions. But leave the results in the Lord's hands. If the other person does not show interest, you may have to accept the hard facts and build other relationships.

Date _____

Day 9

Don't Listen to Some Friends
1 Kings 12:1-19

Key Verses: The king answered the people harshly. Rejecting the advice given him by the elders, he followed the advice of the young men (1 Kings 12:13-14).

Today's Focus:
Rehoboam (probably a teenager at the time) became king of Israel after his father, Solomon, died. The people had worked very hard for Solomon to build the temple. They asked the new king to lighten their labor tasks. Rehoboam asked the elders and some of his friends what to do. He listened to his friends and it caused a civil war.

Read:
Praise God for His great wisdom and understanding.

A. What advice was Rehoboam given by these two groups? Elders of Israel   Rehoboam's Friends

B. How did the people of Israel respond after Rehoboam gave his harsh answer to their request?

C. I need wisdom to discern between good advice and bad advice because:

Need:
Jesus, You are the Good Shepherd. Give me discernment and courage to follow Your leading. My greatest need today is:

God's answer to my prayer came on _____ (date) by this means:

Deed:
My Good Shepherd, lead me to others who are looking for wisdom and guidance. Today, I am looking to encourage someone to follow Jesus regardless of popular opinion. I want to:

Application
Reflect on Psalm 23 concerning how the Good Shepherd will lead you. Why is obeying His guidance and Word so important? If your friends tell you to go against biblical teachings, reject their advice and faithfully follow you Great Shepherd. He will never lead you astray.

Date _____

Day 10

Bad Friends Can Influence You to Do Bad Things
Numbers 16:1-35

Key Verses: Korah son of Izhar, the son of Kohath, the son of Levi, and certain Reubenites – Dathan and Abiram, sons of Eliab, and On some of Peleth – became insolent and rose up against Moses. With them were 250 Israelite men, well-known community leaders who had been appointed members of the council (Numbers 16:1-2).

Today's Focus:
Korah was a priest and important leaders of Israel. He fomented a rebellion against God's appointed leader, Moses. Leaders motivate people to follow them to reach their goals. But their purposes may lead people away from God. Make sure you follow people who are going in the right direction.

Read:
Focus your mind and heart on doing the Lord's will.

A. What did the rebels do that was so bad?

B. Why did Moses become so upset?

C. I want to be a leader who leads people in the right direction because:

Need:
Lord God, I want to follow You wholeheartedly. My greatest need today is:

God's answer to my prayer came on _____(date) by this means:

Deed:
Lord, You are the greatest of all leaders. Lead me to:

Application
The Bible displays leaders of all types – some follow God, some rebel against God; some lead great numbers, some lead only a few. Look through the Bible for men and women who were leaders. Here are just a few to study: Moses, David, Abraham, Paul, Hezekiah, Jehoshaphat, Josiah, Peter, Deborah, and Barnabas. What do you learn from their lives that will help you lead people God's way?

Date _____

Day 11

Praying With Your Heart
Nehemiah 1:1-29

Key Verse: when I heard these things, I sat down and wet. For some days I mourned and fasted and prayed before the God of heaven (Nehemiah 1:4).

Today's Focus:
Nehemiah lived hundreds of miles from away Jerusalem, which had been destroyed by the Babylonians. When he heard of the plight of his people back in Israel, he reacted with deep emotion and concern. He prayed for more than two months that the God of heaven would enable him to rebuild the wall around the city in order to protect the people from hostile neighbors.

Read:
Thank the God of heaven that He has the power and means to help people.

A. What did Nehemiah ask God to do?

B. How did God provide the answer?

C. I am often unaware of the needs of people around me.
   Therefore I want God to:

Need:
Pray that you will sense deeply the needs of others and want to do something about them. My greatest need today is:

God's answer to my prayer came on _____ (date) by this means:

Deed:
Pray for God to show you how to pray more effectively and how to plan wisely to meet the needs that God puts in your heart.

Application
Continue to read about Nehemiah's determination to solve the problems of the Israelites who were living in the destroyed city of Jerusalem. Look at the many kinds of opposition he faced and how he led the people to rebuild the massive wall in 52 days! What did he do to defeat the forces of evil and lead the people to great success?

How can you apply what you have learned about Nehemiah to your life...to your relationships...to your sense of mission?

Date _____

Day 12

Becoming a Peacemaker Rather Than a Troublemaker
James 3:1-18

Key Verse: Peacemakers who sow in peace raise a harvest of righteousness (James 3:18).

Today's Focus:
A peace-loving person is far more attractive than a person who sows discord. We can tame animals, but we have difficulty taming our tongues. How we talk reveals our hearts and attitudes. Wisdom from God produces peace-loving, considerate, merciful, impartial, and sincere behavior.

Read:
Praise the Lord that He can give you the power to control your tongue:

A. What does an undisciplined tongue produce?

B. Contrast two types of wisdom and what they produce:

"Wisdom from the World | Wisdom from Heaven

C. I will seek wisdom from God because:

Need:
Pray that the Lord will make you a peacemaker. My greatest need today is:

God's answer to my prayer came on _____ (date) by this means:

Deed:
Pray for opportunities to exhibit wisdom to others. Based upon godly wisdom, I want to: Here is my plan:

Application
Spend time with God asking Him to reveal in you the areas of worldly wisdom and godly wisdom. Write down the areas that need to change. Do a word study on each word listed in verse 17 by searching the rest of the Bible and a Bible dictionary or concordance.

Date _____

Day 13

Open Your Heart and Then Your Home
Acts 16:1-15

Key Verse: One of those listening was a woman named Lydia, a dealer in purple cloth from the city of Thyatira, who was a worshipper of God. The Lord opened her heart to respond to Paul's message (Acts 16:14).

Today's Focus:
When your life is transformed by the Lord you will want to help others as you have been helped. Lydia, a businesswoman in the Macedonian (Greece) city of Philippi, met Paul and his companions. She experienced a change in her life that affected how she related to other believers.

Read:
Praise God for the changes He has made in your life.

A. Lydia met these strangers and eventually invited them into her home for food and rest. What brought about this dramatic change?

B. Why do you think Paul and his companions went to her home?

C. I want to offer to others what God has blessed me with because:

Need:
Thank the Lord for the material things and Christian friendships He has given you. My greatest need today is:

God's answer to my prayer came on _____ (date) by this means:

Deed:
Pray to give generously to others. Because the Lord has changed my life, I want to:

Application
You may have blessings from God that vary from married adults' blessings. You may be able to open your home to other single adults who are financially strapped or in physical need. You may have clothes, food, transportation, and time to offer to others. List the names of people whom you could help. Ask God for ways you can use your blessings to meet their needs. Read 1 John 3:16-18.

Date _____

Day 14

Encourage Each Other
Philemon 1-25

Key Verse: Your love has given me great joy and encouragement, because you, brother, have refreshed the hearts of the saints (Philemon 17).

Today's Focus:
Paul was in prison in Rome and wrote this letter to his friend encouraging him to forgive Onesimus, a runaway slave. He urged Philemon to do the right thing in God's eyes. We need to encourage one another often to grown in our walks with the Lord and to do the right things.

Read:
Thank God for believers who encourage and motivate you to follow Christ.

A. List some of the words Paul used to describe his friend.

B. What did Paul say should motivate Philemon to receive back Onesimus?

C. I want to become an encouraging person because:

Need:
Lord, I pray that I will do today the things I know are right: My greatest need today is:

God's answer to my prayer came on _____ (date) by this means:

Deed:
Pray to find ways to encourage one another. Because God's eternal life is in me, I want to:

Application
Write down all the names of your friends (single and married) who need encouragement. Then, beside each name, list ways to do this. For example, you might write an email to one, visit another, offer prayer and understanding, or just listen. Also, begin to ask them for their prayer requests so you will know their needs. Read Acts 20:1-6; Romans 15:1-13.

Date _____

Day 15

Handling Loneliness
Luke 10:25-37

Key Verse: But a Samaritan, as he traveled, came where the man was; and when he saw him, he took pity on him (Luke 10:33).

Today's Focus:
Loneliness is one of the major feelings single adults have. Even in a crowd, a person can feel alone. If you get hurt or become sick so that you have to miss work, who would you call? If you were to get into financial trouble or become depressed, who would know? Good friends can help.

Read:
Praise the Lord that He will never leave you.

A. What were the reactions of these three people who came across the wounded, lonely man?

Priest

Levite

Samaritan

B. What did Jesus say were the greatest commandments?

C. How did the Samaritan fulfill both of them?

D. Because I want to be like the Samaritan man, I will:

Need:
Dear Jesus, give me strength to be more caring. My greatest need today is:

God's answer to my prayer came on _____ (date) by this means:

Deed:
Pray to be sensitive to others who are in need. Which of your friends is going through a time of loneliness or pain? Are there others you know who need help?

Application
Think about some other singles that need your encouragement. List ways you can reach out to them. For example, set up a plan for your Bible study group, Sunday school class, or ministry to contact those who miss a meeting. Get people in your church or community to help those who live alone. Invite those who have nowhere to go on holidays to your home or social gathering. Loneliness is minimized as you reach out to others.

Singles and Relationships

Section #2 – Going Deeper Level in Your Relationships

Days 16-31

Date _____

Day 16

Getting Along with Different People
Romans 12:1-8

Key Verses: We have different gifts, according to the grace given us (Romans 12:6).

Today's Focus:
You are uniquely designed and gifted by the Creator. No two people in the world are alike. God has richly given you your special set of gifts so you will fit in with other believers to build up the whole church. Your responsibility is to develop and use these gifts for God's glory.

Read:
Thank the Lord for the gifts He has given you.

A. The choice you have is to keep your life or give it to God. Why does the apostle Paul urge you to do the latter?

B. Because each of us is a part of the whole body, how must we work together?

C. Because I am so grateful for what God has given me, I want to:

Need:
Dear God, I want to know what my gifts are and how to use them wisely. My greatest need today is:

God's answer to my prayer came on _____ (date) by this means:

Deed:
Pray that God will help you humbly work well with others.

Application
Because we all have different gifts, working together is sometimes difficult. Study the different gifts and talents, and ask God to give you wisdom to relate to others who are very different from you. Take a spiritual-gift test to better understand yourself and how to work with others. You can find these kinds of evaluation at (www.TheSinglesNetwork.org) on the Internet or in Christian bookstores.

Date _____

Day 17

Getting Along With Difficult People
Romans 12:9-21

Key Verses: Do not repay anyone evil for evil. Be careful to do what is right in the eyes of everybody. If it is possible, as far as it depends on you, live at peace with everyone (Romans 12:17-18).

Today's Focus:
Because we are all different, we have different motives and various ways of behaving. It's fun to be with people you like, but it's very painful to relate with people who upset you or who act mean. Learning how to treat all kinds of people is at the center of how God wants us to interact.

Read:
Praise the Lord Jesus for showing us how to live.

A. List the ways we should treat others.

B. What will result in overcoming evil with good?

C. I am thankful to God because:

Need:
Lord, I pray to learn to honor others above myself. My greatest need today is:

God's answer to my prayer came on _____ (date) by this means:

Deed:
Pray for those who have hurt you. Because of my salvation and my relationship with Christ, I will:

Application
Reread the passage and place your name or personal pronoun in each sentence. For example, read verse 9 like this: "My love must be sincere. I should hate what is evil; cling to what is good." After you have finished, pray about people who have hurt you. They may include an ex-spouse, parents, girlfriends or boyfriends, friends, coworker, neighbors, or children. List their names and what they have done to hurt you. Write out verses 17 through 21, and sincerely ask God for a change in your heart and attitude toward those people.

Date _____

Day 18

We All Have The Same Purpose
Ephesians 4:1-16

Key Verse: Instead, speaking the truth in love, we will in all things group up into him who is the Head, that is, Christ (Ephesians 4:15).

Today's Focus:
Relationships can stretch us. We can get very impatient with each other, sometimes even losing our tempers. Because of our calling from God, we all have one common goal – to develop our gifts and blend them together to build up the whole body of Christ. This takes humility and love.

Read:
Thank God that you are part of the body of Christ.

A. What are the common things that all believers in Christ possess?

B. How can we work together to build up the body of Christ?

C. Because I want to live a life worthy of the calling I have received, I will:

Need:
Pray that Christ will teach you how to build unity among believers you know. My greatest need today is:

God's answer to my prayer came on _____ (date) by this means:

Deed:
Pray to speak the truth in love. Because unity in Christ, who is our Head, is the goal for all believers, I will:

Application
Sometimes you can become isolated from others and only have superficial relationships. As a result, you're not able to practice patience and develop unity in the Spirit with others. List ways you can grow in these areas (i.e., get involved in a Big Brothers/Big Sisters-style program to help children, visit nursing homes, teach a Bible study, get more involved with your neighbors, etc.). Read Proverbs 19:11; 25:15, Ecclesiastes 7:8, and Colossians 1:11.

Date _____

Day 19

Don't Pattern Your Relationships
Ephesians 4:17-32

Key Verse: So I tell you this, and insist on it in the Lord, that you must no longer live as the Gentiles do, in the futility of their thinking (Ephesians 4:17).

Today's Focus:
Everywhere you turn (TV, movies, Internet, E-mail spam, magazines, newspapers, etc.), the actions and attitudes portrayed as "normal" are against the principles found in God's Word. It's your choice – the world's way or Christ's way. Each of them has consequences.

Read:
Thank the Lord Jesus that He shows us how to live and gives us the power to do His will.

A. Compare the two ways of living and their consequences.

   World's Way

   God's Way

B. What changes does God want you to make in your behavior?

Need:
Ask the Lord to get rid of any bitterness, rage, or anger in your heart. My greatest need today is:

God's answer to my prayer came on _____ (date) by this means:

Deed:
Pray to speak wholesome words to build others up. Many people are still living in the worldly way. I want the Spirit of God to lead me to:

Application
God loves to see you grow in Him. When you make wrong decisions He wants you to return to Him and put away your bad behavior. And He wants you to treat others with love and consideration. Love is patient and motivates us to grow in unity and to work together. Reread the passage and write down the characteristics of a person who builds others up. Note: Encourage you to read "Intentional Relationships for Singles" as your next study.

Date _____

Day 20

We All Need Kind Correct—But Do You Want It?
2 Corinthians 7:1-13

Key Verse: Even if I caused you sorrow by my letter, I do not regret it. Though I did regret it – I see that my letter hurt you, but only for a little while – yet now I am happy, not because you were made sorry, but because your sorrow led you to repentance (2 Corinthians 7:8).

Today's Focus:
Giving kind correction isn't easy, but it produces godly sorrow and needed change if the other person receives it with a desire to improve. But the giver needs to be teachable to receive correction.

Read:
Thank the Lord that He wants you to become holy.

A. How did Paul show the Corinthians he loved them?

B. How did they respond to Paul's first letter?

C. I desire to be mature in Christ, so I will:

Need:
Ask God to teach you His truth. My greatest need today is:

God's answer to my prayer came on _____ (date) by this means:

Deed:
Pray for others who need the Father's wisdom. Today I will seek to give kind correction – as well as to be teachable to receive it.

Application
The Bible has a lot of negative statements about those who gossip and sow discord. Re-read Paul's comments about how to give kind correction and for what purpose. Have you ever been criticized by someone in an unloving or demeaning manner? Well, don't act like that to anyone else. Read and apply to your life Hebrews 12:1-13 and James 1:19-25.

Date _____

Day 21

Forgiven So You Can Forgive
Matthew 18:21-35

Key Verses: the Peter came to Jesus and asked, "Lord, how many times shall I forgive my brother when he sins against me? Up to seven times?" Jesus answered, "I tell you, not seven times, but seventy-seven times" (Matthew 18:21-22).

Today's Focus:
Relationship can never grow without the parties' being able to forgive each other as Christ forgives us. He forgave us and set us free to love Him.

Read:
Praise the Lord because He forgave us first.

A. Contrast the characteristics of the people in the parable.
      King | Servant

B. Why did the king call the servant "wicked"?

C. Because Jesus forgives me, I am willing to:

Need:
Ask Christ to expand your understanding of what He did for you on the cross. My greatest need today is:

God's answer to my prayer came on _____(date) by this means:

Deed:
Pray to forgive those who have hurt you. Because God in Christ has forgiven me of all my sins, I will:

Application:
Forgiving someone is not a one-time event. Christ wants us to forgive each other often. Study forgiveness throughout the Bible to get God's viewpoint. Start with these passages: Psalms 32, 51, 103; Matthew 6:1-15; Luke 17:1-10; Ephesians 4:32, and Hebrews 9. Are there people in your life that you need to forgive? What is stopping you? Ask Christ to make you willing to forgive. Then take the next steps to forgive as God in Christ forgave you.

Date _____

Day 22

What Do You Have in Common?
Romans 14:1-23

Key Verse: Let us therefore make every effort to do what leads to peace and to mutual edification (Romans 14:19).

Today's Focus:
It's fun to interact with others who share your interests and values. But what about people who do things that bother or even disgust you? Accepting them as they are, regardless of how different they are to you, means you are looking for the common basis for your lives. God is an infinitely creative Creator.

Read: Praise the Lord for the way He has made us.

A. In Paul's time one separator of the believers was what they ate. Some people were saved out of paganism that sacrificed bulls to idols. Eating those grilled steaks bothered some Christian believers, but not others. What were the issues that were causing strife among the believers.

B. Why should you related to all believers in Christ?

C. Because God wants me to work for peace with other believers, I will:

Need:
Pray for harmony among your friends. My greatest need today is:

God's answer to my prayer came on _____ (date) by this means:

Deed:
Pray for common ground with others in Christ. I want the Lord to use me to make others feel wanted and part of the group of believers by:

Application
Single adults are diverse as to their life situations, ages, backgrounds, interests, and personalities. Take the initiative to build acquaintances and friends. List some individuals in your life that you would like to get to know better. Endeavor to involve them in planning fun activities, mission projects, and community service to build togetherness.

Date _____

Day 23

It's What You Have Right Now That Counts
Philippians 4:1-20

Key Verse: I know what it is to be in need, and I know what it is to have plenty. I have learned the secret of being content in any and every situation, whether well fed or hungry, whether living in plenty or in want (Philippians 4:12).

Today's Focus:
The Bible doesn't promise you "happiness" or that all your desires will be fulfilled. God says you can be content and enjoy life regardless of your situation. So here's the secret of contentment: be thankful for what you have, not what you don't have.

Read:
Rejoice in whatever situation you are in right now.

A. How can you experience the peace of God?

B. What did Paul's friends in Philippi do for him?

C. Because God is with me and gives me strength, I can:

Need:
Ask God to fill you with contentment and rejoicing. My greatest need today is:

The God of peace met my need on _____ (date) in this way:

Deed:
Pray to help others like the Philippians helped Paul. God can give the strength to face circumstances with contentment and peace. These are the people I would like to talk with about how the Lord can provide what they need:

Application
Paul learned to find contentment even when he was alone. But he also developed loyal friends who knew his needs and tried to meet them. People don't like to be around someone who complains, whines, or acts depressed all the time. Study the words rejoice, joy, thankfulness and faith. Then focus on the fruit of the Spirit in Galatians 5:22-23.

Date _____

Day 24

A Whole New Dimension to Your Love
1 Corinthians 13:1-13

Key Verse: And now these three remain: faith, hope and love. But the greatest of these is love (1 Corinthians 13:13).

Today's Focus:
When Paul writes about love, marital status is not the issue. His life was filled with faith, hope, and love – even though he went through many trials and difficulties. You don't have to be married to experience this quality of love.

Read:
Praise the Lord that He loves you unconditionally.

A. List the characteristics of God's kind of love found in 1 Corinthians 13.

B. Because God showed me unconditional love through Christ, I can:

Need:
Ask God to make you love like that described in 1 Corinthians 13. My greatest need today is:

God's answer to my prayers came on _____ (date) by this means:

Deed:
Pray that your love for others will be patient, kind, joyful, humble, and persevering. The love that God has poured into me through Christ is not just for me. He is motivating me to share that love with others. Therefore, I will:

Application
Love isn't just words. Love is displayed in attitudes, actions, and selfless sacrifice. Look at 1 Corinthians 13:4-8 again. Read the passage out loud and substitute the word God for the word love. Reread the verses and substitute your name for the word love. Ask God to make those words true of your love for others.

Date_____

Day 25

Become a Peacemaker
1 Corinthians 1:1-17

Key Verse: I appeal to you, brothers, in the name of our Lord Jesus Christ, that all of you agree with one another so that there may be no division among you and that you may be perfectly united in mind and thought (1 Corinthians 1:10).

Today's Focus:
Each of us is a unique cluster of strengths, weaknesses, talents, gifts, personality, attitudes, habits, and behavior. God wants us individually to develop ourselves and grow to maturity. Yet every believer in Christ has the common heritage of salvation, fellowship, and the indwelling presence of the Holy Spirit. It is God's intention that we live in harmony.

Read:
Praise the Lord He will keep you strong to the end.

A. What do all believers have in common?

B. What does Christ send us to do?

C. Because God does not want us to have divisions and quarrels, I want to:

Need:
Tell Christ you are eagerly waiting for His return. My greatest need today is:

God's answer to my prayer came on _____ (date) by this means:

Deed:
Pray that the Lord will make you a peacemaker with your friends and church.

Application
The goal of relationships is not who wins an argument or who is the focus of attention. Harmony is the goal – love and respect for each other. This covenant of love is based on Christ and the mission to preach the gospel so people are changed. Because you are not bound to anyone through marriage, it's much easier to get frustrated with each other and leave to go somewhere else. Remember Christ has bound you with each other through His new covenant. Reread Ephesians 4 and Romans 15. Write down ideas you discover on this topic and share it with your friends.

Date _____

Day 26

Reconciliation Is Hard, But The Right Thing
Acts 13:4-12; 15:36-41; Colossians 4:7-10

Key Verse: My fellow prisoner Aristarchus sends you his greetings, as does Mark, the cousin of Barnabas. (You have received instruction about him; if he comes to you, welcome him.) (Colossians 4:10).

Today's Focus:
On their first missionary journey, Paul and Barnabas took along Barnabas's young cousin John (also called Mark). Then when they were planning to go back to the churches they had started, they disagreed so decisively about Mark that they decided to split their relationship. But years later, Paul had totally changed his mind and heart about Mar. Christians may disagree, but reconciliation is the right thing.

Read:
Paris God that He has reconciled you to Himself.

A. How did Paul and Barnabas react to their differences?

B. How did Paul reconcile the situation?

C. I may disagree with other believers, but I will:

Need:
Pray for the courage to admit wrong decisions and ask for forgiveness. My greatest need today is:

God's answer to my prayer came on _____ (date) by this means:

Deed:
Pray for the courage to reconcile strained relationships.

Application
When we humble ourselves before God and ask for His forgiveness. He is faithful to reconcile us with Himself (see 1 John 1:5-9). But Christians may not be so responsive. You cannot determine someone else's reactions when you seek reconciliation. The most important issue is your heart and attitude regardless of the response you receive from someone. Study 1 Corinthians 5:1-6:11.

Date _____

Day 27

Two Kinds of Friends — Love the One and Shun the Other
3 John 1-14

Key Verse: Dear friend, do not imitate what is evil but what is good. Anyone who does what is good is from God. Anyone who does what is evil has not seen God (3 John 11).

Today's Focus:
Eventually what is inside the heart of a person will come out in their statements and behavior. The person who believes the truth about Christ will demonstrate His qualities. A divisive person may disrupt the unity of believers. Honor the doer of truth and disregard the carrier of evil.

Read:
Thank Jesus that He is the way, the truth, and the life.

A. Contrast these two men:
   Gaius | Diotrephes

B. How should you respond to people like Gaius? To people like Diotrephes?

Need:
Ask the Lord to develop in you the same attitudes and actions that Gaius displayed. My greatest need today is:

God's answer to my prayer came on _____(date) by this means:

Deed:
Be thankful for people who act like Gaius. Take the initiative today to show appreciation for individuals who live by God's truth and build up believers.

Application
Do you know how discouraging it is to work to spread God's love and truth but never see results? Gather some friends and plan to do something to honor a specials person who has impacted lives with God's truth. List ideas such as a party, a plaque, or a tribute. Give something with the signatures of all the people that person has influenced for good, such as a signed card or a framed photo. Be creative.

Date _____

Day 28

Mental and Physical Discipline Can Produce Holy Living
1 Thessalonians 4:1-12

Key Verses: It is God's will that you should be sanctified; that you should avoid sexual immorality; that each of you should learn to control his own body in a way that is holy and honorable, not in passionate lust like the heathen, who do not know God (1 Thessalonians 4:3-5).

Today's Focus:
Of all the sins that you might commit, the one that will destroy the working of God in your life and relationships more than any other is sexual immorality. The world portrays immorality as normal and glamorous, but God says it's evil and will be punished.

Read:
Praise God He can teach you to love one another.

A. What should your ambition be, based on today's key verse?

B. Because I desire to do God's will, I will:

Need:
Pray to please God in every aspect of your life. My greatest need today is:

God's answer to my prayer came on _____ (date) by this means:

Deed:
Pray to establish boundaries in your relationships that are holy and honorable. How you treat someone of the opposite sex shows your internal commitment either to the world or to God. I choose to obey God because:

Application
Read what Jesus says about sexual immorality in Matthew 5:27-30 and what Paul writes in 1 Corinthians 6:12-20. Do you struggle with sexual temptation? If so, ask a friend, pastor, or counselor to help you get victory in this battle. Ask a friend or group to hold you accountable to holy living and righteousness.

Date _____

Day 29

Overflowing Joy in Giving
2 Corinthians 8:1-15

Key Verses: Out of the most severe trial, their overflowing joy and their extreme poverty welled up in rich generosity. For I testify that they gave as much as they were able, and even beyond their ability (2 Corinthians 8:2-3).

Today's Focus:
The Macedonian believers were in poverty, yet they responded generously to the needs of the believers in Jerusalem. In fact, Paul asked them not to give so much. But they continued to give. In the same way, God wants us to empathize with other believers in need and give with outrageous joy.

Read:
Praise the Lord Jesus that He gives us joy.

A. Paul explains two examples of giving. What did they give and what were their attitudes?
    Macedonians | Lord Jesus Christ

B. What was Paul urging the Corinthian believers to do? Why?

C. I want to give to others because:

Need:
Humbly ask the Lord to enable you to give like He gave and like the Macedonian believers gave. My greatest need today is:

God's answer to my prayer came on _____ (date) by this means:

Deed:
Give to the people who love God. I want to be wise and filled with God's love when I give my talent, time, and treasure. I want the Lord Jesus to:

Application
Did you know that Jesus talked more about money than He did about heaven, hell, and eternity combined? The Bible is filled with verse about money and possessions. Read Matthew 6:19-21. Treasure refers to your money, your time, your spiritual gifts, your experience – whatever God have given you that will help others. Where you place your treasure reveals your heart. Giving is really grace giving – God has given so much to you that you want to cheerfully give back to Him.

Date _____

Day 30

Hang in There for the Long Haul
Jude 17-25

Key Verses: But you, dear friends, build yourselves up in your most holy faith and pray in the Holy Spirit. Keep yourselves in God's love as you wait for the mercy of our Lord Jesus Christ to bring you to eternal life (Jude 20-21).

Today's Focus:
Getting together on a regular basis for Bible study and fellowship is tough. There are so many conflicting interests, pressures, and busy schedules. What will motivate your group to continue gathering in order to grow closer? The same purposes. Tenacious commitment. Lots of prayer. Desire to study the Bible. The glue for all this is God's love.

Read:
Thank God our Savior that e is all powerful and wise.

A. If your group wants to grow together as well as grow in the Lord, what likely opposition will you face?

B. Why do we need each other in the battle?

Need:
Pray for perseverance regardless of the distractions. My greatest need today is:

God's answer to my prayer came on _____ (date) by this means:

Deed:
Pray to build others up in the faith. Maintaining a relationship is never easy, but it is worth the effort. Since I need to put more energy into building up my friends, I will:

Application
Faith in action and faithful prayer will keep you on course. The enemies of God are always around, trying to make you stumble, to divide believers, and to frustrate Christians' loving each other. Ask the Holy Spirit to make you sensitive to others who are under the enemy's attack. Determine to keep demonstrating God's grace and love for each other. Read and pray to apply Ephesians 6:10-20 each day. And remember 1 John 4:4.

Date _____

Day 31

When the Heat Comes, Fire Up!
1 Peter 4:1-19

Key Verse: If you are insulted because of the name of Christ, you are blessed, for the Spirit of glory and of God rests on you (1 Peter 4:14).

Today's Focus:
Christ as changed you. The temptation will be to go back to the old ways and the old sins. Your old friends may laugh at you and call you names. Your coworkers may make you the topic of gossip and slander. Your relatives may misunderstand. Don't go back. Forge ahead with your new life in Christ.

Read:
Thank Christ that He suffered to give you new life.

A. Contrast the lives of unbelievers with believers:
   Unbelievers; Behavior | Believers' Behavior

B. What should we continue to do regardless of the opposition?

C. I desire to live the way God wants me to live because:

Need:
Seek God's strength to aggressively follow Him. My greatest need today is:

God's answer to my prayer came on _____ (date) by this means:

Deed:
Pray for your friends who are suffering for Christ. I'll use my gifts today to serve other believers. I'll figure out what I can do for someone – and just do it!

Application
When someone crosses from the darkness of the world into the light of God, he or she will be misunderstood by those still in the dark. When the heat of opposition is turned up, the temptation is to wilt. Fire up for the Lord! Pray for each other. Suffer together for Christ's sake. Stand firm in your commitment to fellow believers and to the gospel. Remember, your reward comes from God Himself. Read 1 Corinthians 3:10-15 and 2 Timothy 2:1-13.

Keep Going – *and* Growing

Now that you have established a habit of spending time each day with God, don't slow your progress. Move forcefully ahead for another 31 days. Continue to grow in your knowledge of God and His Word.

Do your best to present yourself to God as one approved, a workman who does not need to be ashamed and who correctly handles the Word of truth (2 Timothy 2:15).

Your relationship will continue to grow as you spend time in the Word, increasing knowledge, affirmation, and reliance. God has so much to give you. He wants you to have the types of relationships that help you grow toward Him.

Additional Scripture to Help You Build Relationships
God's Word gives us so many lessons about building and strengthening relationships. God wants us to have joyful, committed relationships. He wants our relationships with one another to be modeled after His relationship with the church. Whether it's with a person you're dating, your parents, your friends, your children, neighbors, or your coworkers, your relationships need God as the common foundation that causes us to desire unity and harmony. Below is another month's supply of significant Scripture passages for building godly, enriching relationships.

Just like you did during this 31-Day Experiment, spend time each day with your wonderful Lord by studying the Bible, recording your thoughts, and praying for God to work mightily in your life and relationships.

a. Choose one of the verses from the passage you read each day.

b. Write it down on an index card, post it on your Facebook page, your computer and/or smart phone.

c. Think about it all day long and memorize it.

d. Use the guidelines given in the beginning of this book. Learn all you can about how you can trust God to do great things in your life. Ask Him to transform your relationships to conform to His will and purposes.

Day	Passage	Lesson
1.	Luke 15:1-32	Take time to celebrate with each other through good and bad times.
2.	Exodus 18:1-27	Respect your parents and other wise, older people. Spend time with them, honoring their knowledge and wisdom. Desire to learn from their experiences and advice.
3.	John 15:1-17	When we love and obey Christ, we are His friends.
4.	Acts 12:1-19	Pray a lot with your friends and ask God to minister deeply in their lives. Together, believe Him for great things. Tell each other when God has answered prayer so that you may all rejoice together.
5.	2 Corinthians 1:1-11	As you have experienced comfort from God in tough times, comfort each other. Support your friends as they support you.
6.	Romans 15:1-13	Accept one another as Christ has accepted you.
7.	1 John 5:1-12	Knowing Christ secures your place in heaven. Encourage one another to believe the testimony that God has given in His Son.
8.	1 John 2:1-14	If you say you love God and hate your brother, you walk in darkness.

9.	John 19:19-37	Even while Christ hung on the cross, He thought of His mother who was single. He was concerned for her welfare. Demonstrate the same kind of commitment to other people that God puts on your heart.
10.	Job 2:1-13	Sometimes our friends who are hurting just want us to listen and empathize. Come together in agreement as friends to help in time of need.
11.	1 Corinthians 6:1-20	Our bodies are for the Lord, not for sexual immorality. Sexual immorality is one of the quickest ways to destroy a relationship.
12.	Luke 6:46-49	Build relationships on God's Word and truth in order for them to be successful.
13.	1 Corinthians 10:1-13	Temptation is common to all people, even to friends of yours who look like they have everything under control. We all need to trust God for the strength to take the way out that He provides.
14.	Exodus 20:1-17	To live God's way, motivate each other to obey the Ten Commandments.
15.	Ephesians 6:10-24	Fight against evil with the provision God gives you, and learn to live a life of peace with each other.
16.	Philippians 2:1-11	Do not be selfish, but consider others better than yourself.
17.	Colossians 2:1-15	Protect one another from deception, by focusing on Christ.
18.	1 Corinthians 5:1-13	Be careful with whom you associate, as they can cause you to fall.
19.	Luke 10:1-24	Join together to share the gospel with those who don't believe in the Lord Jesus. As you face opposition, encourage each other to be bold for the gospel.

20.	Luke 16:1-15	God knows your heart. You can fool others, but not the Lord. Build up friends and treat people with kindness. Don't trust in money. Trust in the Lord.
21.	1 Thess 5:1-11	Share God's Word together and encourage each other as to the mysteries of the future. Strengthen other believers to walk in the light of Christ.
22.	1 Timothy 3:1-13	Aspire to lead people with respect and integrity, serving believers.
23.	Colossians 1:1-14	Keep growing in your faith. Pray this prayer for each other.
24.	2 Corinthians 5:11-21	God has reconciled us to Himself. How wonderful! Now He has given us the ministry of reconciliation so we can lead others into a life-changing relationship with God.
25.	James 4:1-12	By now you know that when you build friendships with the world, you become an enemy of God.
26.	1 Thess 2:1-16	Do what Paul did to encourage and comfort one another.
27.	Philippians 1:1-11	Share God's blessings with others, and pray earnestly for them.
28.	1 Samuel 20:1-42	Build a friendship that will last through the pressures and threats of life. Trust and loyalty are priceless.
29.	2 Corinthians 6:1-18	Do not cause each other to stumble, but be bound to those who walk with God in righteousness and courage.
30.	Colossians 3:1-17	Treat each other with compassion and kindness. Let Christ's peace rule your hearts and lives.
31.	Ephesians 1:1-23	Thank God for your friends, and pray diligently for them.

The Most Important Thing I *Learned* About Relationships

By Kris Swiatocho

I sat next to my grandmother's chair and watched as she gazed off in the distance at nothing.

I started to rub her back. "How does that feel? Does it feel good?" She closed her eyes and appeared to be enjoying herself, even smiling. I started to sing the only song she could remember, "Silent Night."

She started to sing with me but in Polish, her native language. This would be my last visit, our last memory. She would die two months later in a nursing home in Connecticut while teaching at a church in South Carolina.

This is a bittersweet memory of my grandmother and me because we didn't have a relationship before dementia she developed in her old age. We had spent nearly ten years apart with not even a card between the two of us. Then slowly, as God was changing my heart, I started reaching out to her. It started with a generic card and eventually led me to become her guardian and caregiver. Although she never seemed to change, God would change me.

I started to see my grandmother through His eyes; I began to care for her and provide for her through His provision. I forgave her through His forgiveness of me. I loved her through His love for me.

My grandmother is just one example of how God has changed me through my relationship with Him to help build and strengthen all the relationships in my life. From deepening relationships with friends and family to romantic relationships, all have benefited from spending more time with God and applying His principles.

I look back and can see that it's not so much how others have changed but how I have changed, and as a result, they have started to change. Through Christ, we get our example, our direction, and our strength.

As I travel and minister to single adults and their leaders, there is a common issue of building and strengthening relationships. There seem to be so many obstacles that keep us from developing more robust relationships.

The most important thing I learned about relationships? It's so simple, yet so profound. Every relationship (romantic or platonic) must first start with a relationship with God.

Are you passionate about your relationship with God? Do you know your purpose in life? Do you have a clear understanding of who you are in Christ? Do you value your singleness? Are things that have happened in your past keeping you from developing a solid relationship with God?

Who we are in Christ directly affects how we begin, evaluate, value, and deepen relationships. The Bible speaks about friendships over two hundred times. As our relationship with God grows, it will automatically spill over into our relationships with others. This includes our relationships with who we date, our family, neighbors, and coworkers.

Do you seek friendships that are right in God's eyes? Do you seek friends that encourage you, hold you accountable, and move you toward Christ? Are you spending quality time with your family and friends? Are you communicating with each other? Are you being honest with each other?

If you're seeking a romantic relationship, are you allowing a friendship to precede emotional feelings and then allowing God time to develop that friendship and perhaps enable it to become something more serious? You will never regret having a great friendship with someone you marry. We must seek first to love each other as Christ loves us. And we must work on becoming the right person before we meet the right person.

When I discovered this simple truth, it changed me from the inside out. I began looking to Christ first. He changed my heart and the way I related to other people. I said goodbye to my grandmother, I realized that God had changed me. His way is the right way – the best way.

If You *Want* to Get Married

by Dick Purnell

Are you interested in finding the right person and building a quality relationship? Would you like to develop a friendship that can be the foundation for a strong marriage?

If you do, I have good news for you. Everything we have said in this book can be applied to a right relationship in dating someone. You can build a friendship that leads to a strong marriage.

- Be yourself – don't put on an act just to get the person to like you.

- Ask open-ended questions.

- Listen to the other person's heart, not just their words.

- Treat a woman like a woman. Be sensitive to her feelings and values.

- Respect a man for his character, not his bank account.

- Have fun without negative consequences.

- Become an interesting person.

- Discover how a person makes decisions – if you get married, you will have to make thousands together.

- Talk with a godly, older couple and discover how they built their friendship.

- Seek to understand the other person from his or her viewpoint.

- To accept someone else, you need to accept yourself first.

- Learn to express your heart, not just your head.

- The ability to ask for forgiveness and reconcile is the key indicator of a lasting relationship.

- Everyone needs an emotional refuge.

- Save the physical fireworks for marriage.

- Learn how to caress a person with your words.

- The more you learn about a person, the more you will minimize the negative surprises in marriage.

- Keep your mind pure – it affects everything you do.

- Building spiritual oneness is a lot more than going to church.

- The sure way to destroy a relationship is to make God an add-on.

If you would like to learn more about how to build a relationship that leads to a great marriage, read my book Finding a Lasting Love in which I delve deeper into the above subjects – and many more.

How to Lead a Group of Singles to Experience *Real* Relationships

This 31-Day Experiment about Singles and Relationships according to God's Word can be easily adapted for a group Bible study, Sunday School class, or large group. Whether the group consists of all women, all men, or mixed gatherings of students and/or singles, the participants will be encouraged to grow closer to the Lord and to each other.

Doing this 31-Day Experiment together as a group has many benefits:

1. Everyone will be studying the same passages of Scripture during a month.

2. The whole group will be united together in growing closer to God.

3. People will share their prayer requests with others in the group. Everyone will grow in their faith as members pray for one another and experience God's answering their prayers.

4. Individuals will see how the Lord works in one another's lives.

5. Members can encourage one another in their relationships with the Lord and share their faith in God with other people.

Here are some guidelines to start using *Singles and Relationships* with your group:

1. Remind the people of the purpose of your group – and the need to deepen their relationships with the Lord.

2. Introduce the 31-Day Experiment goal – to build a habit of spending 20 to 30 minutes each day with the Lord in Bible study, prayer, and applying God's Word to life.

3. Show how the book fits into the purpose of your group. Share ideas and passages of Scripture to build one another up. Motivate the people to seek to increase their knowledge of God's Word and to pray more effectively.

4. There are 31 days of study. Do the first day together as a group, showing how to do the study. Encourage group members to start on the same day (preferably the next day) so that each person will always be on the same experiment day. If at all possible, try to meet weekly. Therefore, they will have done six days of the experiment when the next meeting occurs.

5. Plan to complete the experiment with your group in five weeks. Each week the group members should start the experiment days after the group meeting. On the day of the weekly meeting, members should not do the day's experiment. Instead, they can spend that day reviewing their notes from the previous six days and thanking the Lord for all He has done in their lives.

6. When the group settles on the day they all want to start the experiment, send an email reminder of the date to each person and a reminder of the date, time, and place for each weekly meeting. Designate one Email address to which people can send Emails about the things they are learning, prayer requests, and answers to their prayers. Send all the emails received to the whole group each day to encourage people to keep doing the experiment. This will help build group unity and spiritual growth.

7. Encourage members to use a Bible dictionary, Bible concordance, or word-study book when they need to understand passages better.

8. Encourage the group to bring their Bibles and Singles and Relationships to each weekly meeting (which should last from one to one-and-a-half hours).

9. When you meet, discuss each day of the previous week's experiment consecutively. Ask people to share what they learned and how it has affected their lives with the group.

10. If your group is large, you may want to divide it into smaller subgroups, preferably five to six people in each group. Ask the people in the group or these smaller subgroups to call one another during the week to see how each person is doing, answer any questions, and pray together on the phone. In this way, each person will receive several phone calls a week.

11. At the conclusions of each group meeting, pray together, praising the Lord for all He has done and asking Him for consistency to do the experiment faithfully each day. Pray that each person will look forward to meeting with the Lord daily and experience His presence in their lives during the week.

12. Use the Weekly Group Participation Outline as a simple format for the weekly meetings.

Weekly Group Participation Outline

Subject: Singles and Relationships

Content: Review the previous six days

Tips for the leader

1. Prepare your lesson early, asking the Holy Spirit to give you ideas on what to teach and how to draw all the people into the discussion. Be creative. Use a variety of ways to communicate, such as videos, music, drama, and objects – whenever it might take to make the lessons meaningful.

2. Start with a group icebreaker as a way of getting to know one another a little better. Free list on www.TheSinglesNetwork.org

3. Begin with the whole group together, interacting on what they learned that week. Or if your group is large, you may want to split up into small groups. This will allow a greater number of people to share about their experiences.

4. Find out what hindrances they encountered as they sought to meet with God each day. Discuss how to discipline yourselves to consistently spend time with the Lord in the midst of hectic schedules.

5. Let everyone give input on the first day's topic before going on to the second day's topic.

Questions for Discussion

1. How did your meeting with God go each day this past week?

2. What did you have to do to set aside the 30 minutes each day?

3. What did you learn about walking with God? Loving God? Obeying God?

4. What answers to prayer did you receive? What are you still praying about?

5. What kinds of response did you receive when you reached out to other people?

Closing

1. Celebrate all that God has done during the past week and share your prayer requests for the coming week.

2. Discuss the week ahead and the passages you will be studying. Build interest and excitement for the new things you will encounter and learn.

3. Close in group prayer. Lead in praising the Lord for His working and in asking Him to draw everyone closer to Himself during the week. (Option to have people form groups of 4 or less for prayer.)

4. Motivate that people to pray earnestly for one another during the week. Remind them to phone others and send E-mails/text about their experiences. Encourage members to share their faith with people who don't know the Lord personally.

At the end of the five weeks of the experiment:

1. Conclude with a special dinner. Build a fun atmosphere.

2. Make the time a celebration of completing the experiment.

3. Focus attention on the Lord and how wonderful He is.

4. Share testimonies of changed lives and healed relationships.

5. Introduce another 31-Day Experiment or other Bible study (suggestion of Jesus, Single Like Me or Intentional Relationships for Singles). Plan for what you will do next to keep growing in faith and building your group fellowship.

6. Motivate the members to invite their friends to participate in the new study. Encourage them to pray for their friends so they might join the group and get involved in growing closer to God.

It's important that your read all of the information prior to starting "Day 1". This information will tell you how the Bible study has been designed, how to get the most out of it, definitions of terms, a covenant and a prayer. In the back, there is a section on how to use this study as a small group, two articles of interest, an additional 31 days of scripture.

Made in the USA
Columbia, SC
23 June 2023